by

Walt Kelly

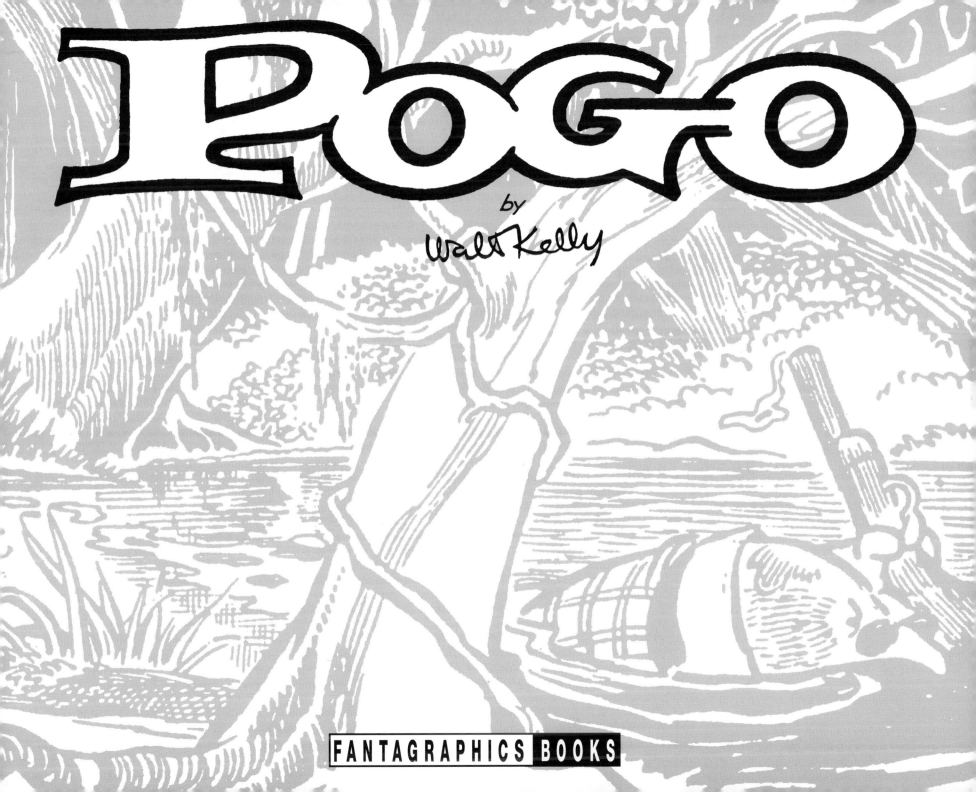

POGO

by

Walt Kelly

FANTAGRAPHICS BOOKS

FANTAGRAPHICS BOOKS

7563 Lake City Way NE
Seattle WA 98115

Edited by Tom Spurgeon
Design and Production by David Lasky
Thanks to Steve Thompson, Bill Blackbeard, and Rick Norwood
for historical and archival assistance
Published by Gary Groth and Kim Thompson

First Fantagraphics Books edition: November, 1998
10 9 8 7 6 5 4 3 2 1

ISBN: 1-56097-324-2

Printed in the U.S.A.

Attacking the Attack Dogs: Walt Kelly's Finest Hour

By R.C. Harvey

"You see, once the dogs are set upon you, everything you have done from the beginning of time is suspect."

This seemingly innocuous statement was found in letters left to his wife and children by Raymond Kaplan, who committed suicide in 1953 because he feared he would be a victim in one of Joseph R. McCarthy's witch-hunting investigations. Kaplan was innocent of any wrong-doing; even the chief dog McCarthy said so after Kaplan had thrown himself under a truck in Boston to end it all. But innocence scarcely mattered in that bleak period of American history known, now, as "the McCarthy Era."

At the risk of heightening the tedium of ho-humdrum here, let me expend forthwith a few paragraphs in reviewing this fearsome phenomenon in American life. Even if you know all about McCarthy and the evil he spawned, reading through the next couple pages will focus your memory and steep you in the brouhahas of the times, thereby preparing you to appreciate all the better what Walt Kelly achieved in *Pogo* in the spring of 1953, the period embraced by this volume's contents.

As we all know full well, McCarthy, the Republican junior U.S. Senator from Wisconsin, gave his name to a particularly virulent brand of unscrupulous know-nothing political chicanery that was the culmination in the early 1950s of over a decade of fear-mongering by legions of self-acclaimed patriots who loudly sought to expose subversive influences at work in America. These influences, it was well-known, aimed with a singular determination at overthrowing the government and undermining the American way of life. Mostly, these influences were either communists or communist-inspired. They had all been identified as "liberals" (or Democrats), according to Republicans. And they were everywhere.

In hindsight, it's not difficult to understand their pervasive presence. During the Great Depression of the 1930s, many politically concerned persons flirted with socialism or communism; capitalism was obviously a failed institution, so it seemed sensible to consider alternatives. For many, the infatuation was short-lived: either the inherent intellectual and practical flaws in communism became apparent, or the need to discover a workable system other than capitalism evaporated when World War II ended the economic blight of the Depression. In any case, the graduates of this particular education were numerous; they were, indeed, everywhere in American life. Moreover, some of them remained committed to communism. In actual fact (not McCarthyist fact), there were some communists working in the government bureaus during the time McCarthy was looking for them. Not many, but some.

As long as Soviet Russia was an ally in World War II, the issue of communist influence in America was scarcely an inflammatory one. But when in the late 1940s the Cold War commenced — when the Soviet Union's ambition to conquer the world was widely advertised — communists were suddenly a "menace." Then in rapid succession, China fell to communism, and Russia acquired nuclear capability. World domination by the Reds all at once seemed a real possibility. And to millions of fearful Americans, it seemed likely that communists had infiltrated the corridors of power in the U.S. State Department and had engineered the collapse of Nationalist China and were probably plotting further mischief. These fears seemed supported by two actual events. A dapper Democrat politician in the State Department named Alger Hiss was found guilty of perjury in a trial alleging that he had sold secrets to the Soviets; and Julius Rosenberg and his wife Ethel were found guilty of giving the atomic bomb formula to Russia. Since the Democrats were in the White House at the time (and had been since 1932), the Republicans, frothing at the mouth to displace their political rivals on the seat of power, seized upon the Red Menace as a device by which Democrats could be discredited. The Democrats, it was alleged, had been too permissive with communists: they had permitted them to take jobs in the State Department and elsewhere where they could effect all sorts of sabotage.

In an attempt to contain the damage,

Harry Truman, as President, had instituted loyalty checks and oaths for government employees. As a means of checking, the Attorney General developed a list of organizations with questionable intentions about the American way of life, and if any government employee's membership in such an organization could be discovered, that employee would be suspect and might be removed from the payroll.

At about the same time, the House of Representatives revived its Committee on Un-American Activities, which joined the National Loyalty Review Board in ferreting out subversives in government. The Committee (known as HUAC, the House Un-American Activities Committee) had been insisting for years that there were communist spies in government. They had found very few, but they had ruined the careers and wrecked the lives of hundreds of innocent people while flushing out the few. The loyalty of some federal employees was questioned for the flimsiest of reasons — past associations with liberal organizations (many long since defunct) on the Attorney General's list, unfounded rumor, accusations of spiteful co-workers, and so on. Then in Kafkaesque hearings, the accused were denied the right to confront their accusers — or, even, to know who their accusers were — because disclosing those identities might compromise investigations in progress. No proof was needed to justify dismissal: if a person's name so much as appeared in a report about merely allegedly suspicious persons, that was sufficient indication of "subversive tendencies," and anyone with such tendencies could expect to be sacked.

The entertainment industry developed a practice equally insidious — blacklisting. Those whose names appeared on these lists were fired not because they were communists or even suspected of being communists: the mere presence of their names on the lists simply made them too controversial for sponsors or producers to handle. No witnesses. No evidence. One actress lost her livelihood because she had the same name as another person whose name appeared on the list.

Joe McCarthy arrived on the national scene just in time to take advantage of the "Red Scare." A wholly unprincipled political opportunist, McCarthy felt his star in Wisconsin was sinking in early 1950 and needed a campaign issue, something that would put him on the front pages of his state's newspapers — and, possibly, on the front pages of newspapers elsewhere, too. After consulting with a couple of advisers, he decided that communists in government was a good issue, and on Lincoln Day in Wheeling, West Virginia, before the Ohio County Women's Club, he made a speech during which he waved a sheet of paper over his head and said it was a list of 205 State Department employees known to be members of the Communist Party (which, in those days, was not at all an illegal affiliation but was certainly a suspicious organization). Five years later, by the time McCarthy had been thoroughly discredited and censured by his colleagues in the Senate, not a single person on this list had been found to be a communist — a circumstance not at all surprising considering that the list itself never really existed. It was a fiction, a prop for McCarthy's political theater. (McCarthy later confessed that the piece of paper that he had held aloft was "an old laundry list.") But that hardly mattered: with his trumped-up list, McCarthy had struck a mindless nerve in the body politic, and the Age of Suspicion had acquired its messiah, a leader of the yelping pack.

McCarthy, a shifty-eyed rogue, a graceless freebooter with a gift for self-promotion, epitomized the Age. He didn't invent McCarthyism, but he raised its techniques to an art form which he then personified. His method was based upon a fundamental disregard for the truth. He proved himself a master of reckless accusation, unabashed equivocation, and outright lying. He determined guilt by association and made liberal use of innuendo and half-truth, not to mention ordinary smearing, character assassination, and — once he was confident of wide-spread support — naked intimidation. When officials questioned his allegations, McCarthy countered by questioning their loyalty and their intentions. Since he, McCarthy, was the champion of the anti-communists, anyone who raised any doubts about him was interfering with his patriotic work, seeking, presumably, to stop him in this noble pursuit. Such persons were clearly either communists or the unwitting tools of communists, McCarthy would say. It was name-calling raised to the nth degree. And those who McCarthy cast such aspersions upon were often unemployed or disgraced shortly thereafter.

The country found itself embarked almost without knowing it upon a mad and feverish course, blown this way and that by the shifting gusts of public opinion, buffeted by fears so unreasoning as to be nearly pathological. In Madison, Wisconsin, reporters from the *Capital Times* composed a petition in the summer of 1951 and walked the streets, asking citizens if they'd sign it. The petition consisted entirely of verbatim quotations taken from the Declaration of Independence and the U.S. Constitution. Virtually no one would sign it. Some said the sentiments expressed in it were obviously subversive. But many gave no reason for their refusal. They were simply frightened into silence, into absolute anonymity. A hothouse incubating sensation and hysteria, the nation fermented menace twenty-four hours a day. Half-baked notions took root quickly; inflammatory accusations blossomed overnight into established "facts." The delirium would become a disease, and the disease a disgrace.

Many people recognized at once that McCarthy was a fraud. On the day after the historic speech in West Virginia, Herblock, the acerbic editorial cartoonist at *The Washington Post*, drew a cartoon of McCarthy in which the senator appeared to be transparent, suggesting strenuously than his charges were pretty thin. (In the next month — on March 29, 1950, to be precise — Herblock coined the term "McCarthyism" in a cartoon that showed an assortment of Republican senators pushing the GOP elephant toward a tower of tar barrels, the uppermost of which was labeled "McCarthyism.") Chairing a committee charged with investigating McCarthy's allegations, Senator Millard Tydings of Maryland issued a report on June 17 that found not a shred of evidence in support of McCarthy's charges; McCarthy was effectively branded a liar.

Earlier that month, on June 1, a fellow Republican senator, Margaret Chase Smith of Maine, rose in the well of the Senate to present to that body a "Declaration of Conscience," signed by herself and six other Republican senators, protesting McCarthy's behavior. She was not proud of "the way the Senate has been made a publicity platform for irresponsible sensationalism," she read; "I am not proud of the reckless abandon in which unproved charges have been hurled." And she did not want her party to ride "to political victory on the Four Horseman of Calumny — Fear, Ignorance, Bigotry and Smear. . . . While it might be a fleeting victory for the Republican Party, it would be a more lasting defeat for the American people."

McCarthy's reaction to these supposed reverses is instructive. About the Tydings report, McCarthy said, "The most loyal stooges of the Kremlin could not have done a better job of giving a clean bill of health to Stalin's fifth column in this country." Tydings was giving "aid and comfort" to the enemies of the United States. And McCarthy's response to the Declaration of Conscience was similar. Speaking in the Senate, he said, "Let me make it clear to the administration, to the Senate, and to the country that this fight against communism shall not stop, regardless of what any group in this Senate or in the administration may do." The patriot was undaunted and undeterred.

At just about this time, the southern half of Korea was invaded by the northern half, and the U.S. was faced with fresh communist threat. McCarthy's crusade was consequently re-vitalized even as its leader was thoroughly discredited by his colleagues.

So how did he survive? Not only survive — but thrive?

McCarthy survived because he was a genius at manipulating the news media. He understood, apparently, that the press was a knee-jerk institution. "News is news" in every city room in the country, whether in the print or broadcast medium. McCarthy was a high-ranking elected government official, and when he made one of his accusations, it was news. Whether it was true or not was irrelevant to the press. McCarthy enjoyed for a time the enthusiastic right-wing support of both Robert McCormick's powerful midwest mouthpiece, *The Chicago Tribune*, and all of the newspapers in

the Hearst chain. But even liberal papers were forced by the customs of the trade to give McCarthy front-page play. In the antique litanies of the journalistic profession, it was axiomatic that news about McCarthy sold newspapers, and if the competing newspaper down the street was screaming with headlines about McCarthy's latest charges, so must every other newspaper shriek with McCarthy news in 72-point type.

McCarthy quickly mastered the techniques necessary to dominate the news. He would call a press conference to announce that he would have a press conference the next day, and the day's papers would carry headlines heavy with proclamatory import: McCarthy Calls Press Conference Tomorrow. And when some allegation of his was proven completely wrong, McCarthy simply shifted his attack and targeted a new victim. The sensation of his new charges drew fresh headlines, displacing stories about his errors. His was the tactic of a guerrilla raider, and he used it time and again with astonishing effectiveness.

Furthermore, compounding the confusion, the press never announced McCarthy's mistakes with headlines as large as those it gave to his accusations. His charges were repeated, day after day, in the nation's newspapers. Every person he accused of being a communist or a communist sympathizer ("comsymp" was the expression) found his or her name on the front pages of papers across the land for days. When the charges proved false, the news was announced in smaller type — and only once. Denials never outshouted accusations; the exposure of charges as false never received the attention given the innuendoes that prompted the initial notice. By a simple process of constant reiteration, McCarthy's lies achieved something of the status of truth. Where there's smoke, goes the folk adage, there must be fire. It was a technique that Joseph Goebbels had perfected in Nazi Germany a generation earlier, the propaganda technique of "the Big Lie." The bigger the lie, the more likely people are to believe that there must be some truth behind it, however small a truth.

Supported by the edifice of self-promotional publicity that he

constructed around himself, McCarthy maintained his political clout. His self-imposed mission to root out communists in government made him a hero to many. He inspired a vociferous following of millions. And as others took up his cause and methods, reputations and livelihoods in every corner of American life were destroyed with little or no regard for the truth. No one, whether in pubic service or private enterprise, was safe from McCarthyism.

McCarthy undertook to revenge himself upon the hapless Tydings, who had served in the Senate for twenty-four years; McCarthy engineered his defeat in the 1950 off-year election by circulating a photograph faked to show Tydings hobnobbing with Communist Party leader Earl Browder. With that, McCarthy assumed among his fellow politicians the stature of a true political power broker. He was a force to be reckoned with. And to be feared. By the end of 1953, he was being tagged as the second most powerful man in the country, President Dwight Eisenhower being the first. McCarthy

was so popular that other politicians, however much they disapproved of the man's techniques, were reluctant to voice their disapproval because that might make them appear "soft on communism" (as McCarthy would say), and in consequence, they might lose their next contest at the polls. If they opposed him, McCarthy might just include their names on his next fabricated list of communist conspirators.

With Ike's election in 1952, however, the GOP leaders in the Senate had actually sought to silence the obstreperous and often embarrassing McCarthy. Or at least to muzzle him. They did it by assigning him to chair an obscure committee, which, they supposed, would render the sensation-seeking senator harmless. This was the Government Operations Committee. But the Party leaders outsmarted themselves. They hadn't reckoned on McCarthy's ingenuity, and they underestimated his audacity. The committee was supposed to concern itself with such mundane matters as auditing financial reports from bureaus and reorganizing departments and, occasionally, investigating graft. For this last purpose, there was a Permanent Subcommittee on Investigations. With fiendish glee (we might suppose), McCarthy seized upon this subcommittee. He saw that its charter permitted it to investigate virtually anything — in government or out. He named himself chairman of the subcommittee and abandoned the main body to another. He had found his perch of power. Under his stewardship, this humble, inconsequential subcommittee would soon steal the spotlight from all other governmental investigative bodies, and McCarthy would be in the center of the stage, eclipsing all the rest — HUAC, the Senate's Judiciary Committee and its Internal Security Committee, not to mention the FBI, CIA, the Treasury Department and the Secret Service, all of whom were also pursuing communists in government and elsewhere with ferocious dedication and trumpeting publicity.

McCarthy quickly hired a new chief counsel, a young man named Roy Cohn, who brought along with him a friend, G. David Schine. Staffed and ready, McCarthy launched his first investigation. Undertaking to see if the Voice of America was infiltrated by communists, McCarthy opened hearings on February 16, 1953, just a month before the *Pogo* strips in this volume started appearing.

McCarthy's agenda that season was scarcely single-minded. He was also objecting to a couple of Presidential nominations — that of an ambassador to Russia and of a high commissioner to Germany. McCarthy lost on both issues but garnered the usual allotment of headlines. And before the dust settled, McCarthy was off on a new crusade, this time alleging that ships supplied by the U.S. to other maritime powers were being used to carry strategic materials behind the Iron Curtain. Before he abandoned this project for another, he had raised the ire of the State Department by conducting independent negotiations with Greece to reduce the shipments (for which, in the natural course of journalistic events, he received front-page coverage).

Other communist-related news of the period included reports of world-wide agitation protesting the execution of the Rosenbergs (which, after yet another delay, finally took place June 20) and the death of Russian dictator Joseph Stalin on March 4, and Owen Lattimore's fight with McCarthy over the latter's charges that Lattimore was a Russian spy who had engineered U.S. far eastern policy, and, hence, caused the loss of China to communism.

The Lattimore case is almost a benchmark of McCarthyism. Lattimore was the first person McCarthy accused by name. On March 21, 1950, after several days of promising to name "the top Russian espionage agent in the United States" — several days of headlines — McCarthy finally named Lattimore, a virtually unknown academic specialist on China. He was not even an employee of the government; he was a college professor who occasionally advised the State Department. And although the professor successfully defended himself repeatedly over the next several years, McCarthy wouldn't let go. He kept discovering new "evidence." None of it, however, was sufficiently persuasive to convince anyone but a publicity-hungry demagogue of Lattimore's guilt. But Lattimore kept being haled up before one investigatory committee or another to testify. In 1952, for example, he testified for days before the Senate's Internal Security Committee. By all reports, it was a brutal episode.

Attempting to read an opening statement, Lattimore was interrupted so often that after three hours he had managed to read only eight lines of it. *The Washington Post* reported: "The subcommittee, with half a dozen members and two staff lawyers, all acting as prosecutors, has been able to question this lone witness in relays. For nine days it has subjected Lattimore to an incessant drumfire of interrogation. . . . It is a frightening spectacle to see a committee of the United States Senate bully and torment a witness in this fashion—as though he were in an arena, at bay, providing sport for the public." The committee refused to give Lattimore time to reflect or think about his answers when asked questions about events that had taken place twenty years earlier, to consult his attorney, or to respond to any question with more than "yes" or "no." The committee was bent on trapping the professor into committing perjury, and he eventually did. Exhausted emotionally and physically, he couldn't help but stumble over a couple inconsequential facts, failing to recall accurately or to report completely some event that had taken place in the misty past.

He was accused of lying on five matters, including denying that he knew that an obscure Chinese official was a communist, claiming that Outer Mongolia was independent (not Soviet controlled) after World War II, and giving an inaccurate description of his relationship with a person who had written about the committee hearings. This was bunk. Under the circumstances of his testimony, Lattimore could be expected (indeed, *was* expected) to make mistakes of this sort. None of the charges were substantial enough to take Lattimore to court, but, plagued by the damage to his reputation, Lattimore hounded the Justice Department to indict him. It finally did, charging that he had lied when he denied being a communist sympathizer. He was not accused of being a communist or an agent of communism. He was, rather, accused of something so vague as to be unprovable. And, in fact, it could not be proven. In May 1953, the case was thrown out of court because the indictment was a violation of the First Amendment.

The Justice Department, however, did not give up on Lattimore. It assembled new "evidence" to show that he was a communist sympathizer — excerpts from the professor's writing taken out of context which showed that, on one occasion or another, for one reason or another, at one time or another, long ago — his views paralleled those of the Communist Party. This indictment, too, was thrown out of court, this time on the grounds that it violated not only the First Amendment but the Sixth, which requires that an accused person be "informed of the nature and cause of the accusation" against him. The charges in this case were, the judge ruled, so vague that no one could determine the nature and cause of the accusations. Finally, on June 28, 1955, all charges against Lattimore were dropped. By then, his case had spanned the entire McCarthy Era.

In the spring of 1953, however, McCarthy was still riding high, and his minions and his actions were claiming headlines daily on the front pages of the nation's papers while on the comics pages, Kelly was moving to conclude his attack on McCarthyism. McCarthy suddenly began claiming that the overseas libraries of the State Department were laced with books by communists or apologists for Soviet Russia, and he sent Cohn and Schine to Europe to investigate. Their antics were avidly covered every day in the press. By June, U.S. libraries were reported to be destroying undesirable books (including those authored by writers who took the Fifth Amendment when questioned by HUAC or other investigatory bodies in government).

McCarthy effectively undermined the Constitutional guarantee of the Fifth Amendment which permits a person to decline to answer questions on the grounds that the answers might be self-incriminating. McCarthy's explanation: "If you ask a man whether he's a communist, and he's under oath; if his answer were to be 'no' — a truthful answer — that would not incriminate him. The only way he could be incriminated would be if he is a communist. So when a man comes before our committee and says, 'I won't answer because if I told the truth I might go to jail,' it means, of course, that obviously he's a communist."

Persons whose livelihoods were destroyed by the suspicions generated by a witch-hunting government numbered in the hundreds, perhaps thousands. A ship's butcher in the merchant marine was fired because the Coast Guard declared him a security risk. He wasn't a subversive himself, but his brothers were "believed" to be "associated with" the Communist Party. Because he said he knew nothing about any of that, the butcher was declared to be "uncooperative," and his dismissal was upheld by the board to which he had appealed his case. In another instance, a plumber lost an employment opportunity because the contractor for whom he worked was subjected to a security clearance investigation before getting a government contract. The plumber, it was determined, was "maintaining a close continuing association with his wife," who was engaged in activities of an organization which was communist, namely the Communist Party. The plumber and his missus were properly aghast since neither had ever been members of the Communist Party or had endorsed any of its ideas. The wife, however, reported that her name had been used on the letterhead of the Spanish Anti-Fascist Refugee Committee (a defunct organization on the Attorney General's list) in about 1938 — albeit without her permission. And she might have donated a few dollars to someone professing to represent a worthy

cause during a cocktail party once. The plumber and his wife were subsequently cleared as security risks, but the clearance took two years to accomplish, and during that time, the plumber's erstwhile employer would not hire him — nor would anyone else in the construction business. His livelihood had been effectively destroyed.

One more example: A radio actress, Madeline Lee, made a living by gurgling like a baby on the air. Accused of having communist associations years before, she was blacklisted in 1953 and could find no further employment in radio. Three other actresses also had their careers destroyed as a result. None were accused of any political activity whatsoever. One lost her job because she had the same name as Miss Lee; another, because she looked like Miss Lee; and the third who neither had the same name nor resembled Miss Lee but was unlucky enough to earn her living by squealing like a baby for radio audiences.

Is it any wonder that Raymond Kaplan took his own life when he thought he might be investigated by McCarthy? He knew from reports of the fates of others that if he were summoned, his ability to earn a living at his profession would end. He no doubt reasoned that he may as well be dead.

McCarthy was by no means laying waste to cherished American freedoms without being criticized. Many newspapers attacked him on their editorial pages — while giving him headlines on their front pages; but nationally prominent political figures (like, for instance, President Eisenhower, who masked his political timorousness by saying he wouldn't get into the gutter with McCarthy) were slow in rising to the challenge. Washington's celebrated muckraker, Drew Pearson, fired a shot or two, and then McCarthy rounded on him, insinuating that Pearson was a tool of Moscow and advising people not to buy the hats manufactured by the sponsor of Pearson's radio program, the Adam Hat Company. Pearson wouldn't be silenced, but he lost his sponsor, who chose not to risk a boycott led by the powerful senator.

Strangely, television journalists were

nearly silent. It is strange today, at least, to imagine a time when TV news organizations were not clamoring for our attention with punditry on both sides of such an issue. But in those days, television, still in its infancy, was seen as a much more powerful medium than either radio or the print press. Its audiovisual impact was immediate and persuasive, but its ability to air complex issues thoroughly and fairly was (and still is) suspect. So TV newsmen (in a demonstration of restraint difficult to believe from the perspective of post-Watergate America) were inclined to stick to the barest of facts. And the evil that McCarthy's critics saw in his method did not reveal itself readily with that kind of treatment.

Finally, Edward R. Murrow, the patron saint of CBS News and one of the most prestigious journalists in the world, attacked McCarthy on March 9, 1954 on his highly regarded "See It Now" program. Murrow's expose alternated film clips of McCarthy making charges and assertions with shots of

Murrow, live, presenting the contradictory facts. The relentless rhythm of lie refuted by truth again and again drummed in the flagrancy of the senator's perfidy. Some said the program was as artfully constructed of half-truths as anything McCarthy had done. Be that as it may, given McCarthy's power, going on the air with any sort of attack, at that time, took guts.

True, the canny Murrow, a finger on the national pulse, had waited until the public was ready to hear some uncomplimentary things about McCarthy before he went on the air. And Murrow

scarcely destroyed the senator with that broadcast, but he nonetheless deserves to be remembered as showing great moral resolve in attacking the senator. The broadcaster thereby secures his honorable spot in the history of journalism. Walt Kelly, we note with considerable pride, went for McCarthy's throat almost a year before Murrow did. McCarthy was then at the pinnacle of his fame and power as the nation's foremost crusader against communists.

Kelly had launched several satirical shafts at the witch-hunting tactics of the anti-communist crusaders, as we've noted in these pages ere now. With many of the journalistic fraternity, he had long ago realized that McCarthy was at least a charlatan and perhaps a monstrous one, spewing the sulphurous fumes of intimidating invective with every press conference. By the spring of 1953, McCarthy was ripe, Kelly saw, as a subject for satirical ridicule.

In later years, Kelly would provide alternative strips for newspapers to run in place of his sharpest satirical ones, should his point-of-view be something the editors deemed offensive to their readers. But in 1953, Kelly showed not only artistic genius in his McCarthy sequence but great courage: given the popularity of McCarthy, Kelly risked cancellation by scores of newspapers whose readers were sympathetic to the senator's crusade.

Kelly, in perfect tune with his self-proclaimed role as the world's oldest boy cartoonist, disagreed on this point. Said he: "One indication of how far fear had been allowed to infiltrate in the days when informers were being considered for high honors came to me at a time when I'd decided to pluck the Malarkey out of the air and put it into the strip. An extremely liberal friend who had not been saying much for quite a while, said, 'You were skating on thin ice when you had that guilt-by-association trial of Albert for eating the Pup-dog (Volume 4). But now, with this Malarkey stuff, you've broken through.'

"It didn't seem to me then, nor does it now [in 1959]," Kelly continued, "that a comic version of senatorial low-jinks was dangerous. Of my then three hundred and fifty editors, not one objected. They'd be the last to think they'd been courageous in running the material. In short, the whole situation might be termed 'over-evaluated.'"

But Kelly, I submit, is over-simplifying and, typically, glossing over the danger with a jibe and a jest. It's a mark of his essential humility not-to-say modesty. The truth of the matter, however, is at least quietly harrowing.

Editorial cartoonists (led by Herblock, whose contribution Kelly commemorated on 5/20 by putting his name on the boat) had skewered McCarthy regularly once the Senator became well known. But syndicated comic strips in those days were still relatively free of political satire. Al Capp made fun of the rigid right, but no one named names. Kelly changed that. And as a cartoonist satirizing a national figure of McCarthy's power in a syndicated strip at the height of the senator's popularity, Kelly ran a greater risk than Murrow (who, as I said, had waited until McCarthy had almost hung himself before coming in to help with the noose).

Kelly's complimentary refrain to the contrary notwithstanding, newspaper editors are notoriously timorous about the features in their papers. They listen to their readers with fear and trembling. Keeping readers happy keeps circulation steady; ditto publishers' incomes and editors' jobs. And it doesn't take many readers objecting to a syndicated feature to convince an editor that he risks losing circulation by provoking certain kinds of controversy. Syndicated features, aiming assiduously for universal acceptance — the greatest possible appeal — are consequently inclined to be studies in the most unobjectionable social fodder imaginable. And McCarthy was still a national hero to huge segments of the populace in the spring of 1953 when Kelly launched his attack. Substantial numbers of readers could have objected to Kelly's satire; and scores doubtless did. The cartoonist, scarcely Murrow's equal except as a mover and shaker, was risking his very livelihood. To their everlasting credit, as Kelly noted, most newspaper editors stuck with him. (Perhaps they didn't realize soon enough that a full-bore satire was shaping up on their comics page, where such things had never appeared be-

fore. But enough: let me grant them the courage of their editorial-page convictions at least.) But Kelly could not have known they would countenance his satire when he started it; in fact, all the evidence of history would have convinced him that they would desert him in droves. The McCarthy sequence in *Pogo* is therefore a ringing testament to the cartoonist's courage. Or, at least, to his admirable audacity.

Before turning to the strips at the right, it might be useful to recall that Howland Owl set himself up a television program in the weeks preceding the contents of this volume. Owl's TV program advertised and attempted to sell "Dirt." Kelly intends us to perceive "dirt," partly, as "gossip" — innuendo and rumor — the sort of pseudo-information McCarthy was so adept at dealing in. (And the word-playing Kelly adroitly turns "columnist" into "calumnist," one who, we assume, traffics in "calumny" — i.e., false statements — on 2/25 and 3/7 in the last volume.) That Kelly sees television as a culpable partner in McCarthyism seems clear.

To create a narrative metaphor for McCarthy's commie hunt, Kelly turned to the swamp's Bird Watchers Club. Kelly established the hapless bat brothers as permanent members of the Club and put the censorious Deacon Mushrat at the head of the bumbling band of would-be witch-hunters. This disreputable bunch is occasionally abetted in their nefarious work by cowbirds, who, realizing how thoroughly they are disliked on all sides, pose as doves (becoming thereby "former" communists whose present behavior and lingo on 3/17 suggest that they haven't altogether abandoned their earlier allegiance — just as, it would be assumed by various investigatory bodies, the one-time communist sympathizers of the 1930s hadn't quite given up communist dreams). The Deacon is then joined by Mole MacCarony, who, despite his handicap (he can barely see), begins a program to purify the swamp of all germs.

"The introduction of Mole MacCarony," Kelly wrote, "was an attempt to find a symbol for another wad of bug-eyed greed which was typified by our sudden worry about who was coming into the country as a refugee or an immigrant and who,

for that matter, was going to be allowed to stay here. Such goings-on became comic fodder when we suddenly wake up and realize that not a single Indian was consulted."

Mole comes to the swamp to help with the spring bird watching (communist hunting). And in portraying Mole as fanatic about sanitary conditions, Kelly perfectly captures the righteous fervor of the witch-hunters. "Bacteria from all over infect the pure air of our land," Mole cries. But Mole's ability to discover impurities is seriously in doubt: the Deacon says (March 4 [3/4], in the previous volume) that Mole has "a keen eye," but Kelly shows him bumping blindly into a tree in the very next panel. Driving home the point on 3/18, Kelly has Mole addressing a stump as if it were Owl, and on 3/19 and 3/23, Mole finds even his own reflection "suspicious." Kelly is pulling no punches: he makes sure we understand that "bird watching" is being conducted by people who aren't very perceptive.

On 3/23, the exchange between Mole and one of the cowbirds (a former communist, remember) echoes the sort of guilt-by-association reasoning at which McCarthy and his cohorts were so adept, invoking, also, the shadow of blacklistings. Mole's supposedly patriotic motive is revealed to be mere mercenary greed on 3/25 — just as McCarthy was motivated by a desire for power, to which publicity was but the means. And on 3/27 and 3/30, Kelly conjures up nightmares of book-burning, evoking perhaps memories of the Nazi regime in the 1930s. By giving Owl a terrified expression on both days, Kelly is clearly hoping we see more in book-burning than heat and light.

On 4/2, Kelly's opening panel word-play reveals the satirical undercurrent he is generating: once again, the "columnist" vs. "calumnist" equation, then a "truth" that can be perceived only by invading privacy (a "keyhole troth," with "trough" suggesting a pig sty through which one must wade to get this sort of "dirt;" and, finally, "peek aboo" about "nothing").

By this time, Mole has emerged as representing something a good deal more sinister than he seemed at first. Starting with an effort to eradicate all germs, he soon moves to rid the swamp of all "impurities," all "migratory birds" — that is, for-eigners (and probably, therefore, communists) — but because he can't see well enough to identify his victims, it isn't long before everyone is under suspicion.

"What kind of an owl are you?" Mole asks Turtle (4/9).

"I ain't no owl," says Turtle. "I ain't even a bird."

"Were you ever a bird, or are you thinking of becoming one?" asks Mole, invoking the ritualistic incantation with which all investigatory bodies initiated their questioning of witnesses. ("Are you now or have you ever been a member of the Communist Party?")

By turns, Kelly gives two of his cast a chance to be heroes and extricate the swamp from the threatening Mole. Albert is Kelly's usual heroic figure (albeit not at all commonsensical like Pogo when the possum is the heroic one), but he is too easily distracted by semantic confusion (4/14-15 and 4/20-21). Porky, on the other hand, enables Kelly to draw a sharp contrast between the traditional role of America and the obviously un-American purposes Mole is aiming for (4/17-18). But Kelly will permit no one to derail his satire at this point, so neither Albert nor Porky is effective against Mole.

Perfect though Mole seems as a satirical vehicle for Kelly's attack on the Red Hunt, the character is too much a buffoon to stand in for the gimlet-eyed senatorial gangster from Wisconsin, who Kelly regards as a frighteningly diabolic figure in American life. He can manipulate Mole for laughs, thereby ridiculing the witch-hunters; but he needs something much more grimly threatening, too.

To this end, Kelly brings in a wild cat named Simple J. Malarkey, "a good wing shot and a keen eye" (5/1). Malarkey gets himself elected president of the Bird Watchers Club by waving his shotgun under Deacon's nose: "Betsey, here," says the leering cat, "got six or seven votes in her alone" (5/6). The reign of terror and intimidation begins. Malarkey, in case you haven't guessed, looks remarkably like Joseph R. McCarthy, and the echo of McCarthy's technique is as clear as the invocation of his name in the syllabic rhythm of the stand-in's name.

Years later (in 1959's *Ten Ever-lovin' Blue-eyed Years with Pogo*) Kelly remembered McCarthy with tongue-in-cheek affection: "There has never been much question in my mind that the man who Simple J. Malarkey represented was one of the great all-time comedians. This is because he was a *true* comedian: he was not pretending for a moment. With his uproarious and highhanded disregard of the amenities and established precedent, he became almost a law to himself. Before our very eyes, we saw ourselves allowing ourselves to be chumps. The man was just great. I miss him. He was completely unpredictable and, therefore, fascinating."

Kelly thought McCarthy was evil, no question; but he also realized that the senator had furnished him with some of the best material he'd yet encountered. By the early 1950s, Kelly had come to understand that, as he put it, "if I were looking for comic material, I would not ever have to look long. We people manufacture it every day in hundreds of ways. The news of the day would be good enough." If, he went on, the "complexion" of the strip changed subsequent to this realization, it was probably because "it is pretty hard to walk past an unguarded gold mine and remain empty handed."

On various editorial pages throughout the land, some perceptive souls recognized that McCarthy was employing methods that had been used to advantage a generation earlier by an Austrian paperhanger and his gang in Nazi Germany. Kelly recognized a thoroughly American antecedent in the Ku Klux Klan, an understanding he permitted to surface in the strip (5/23), doing his best to show that members of the KKK were no better equipped to show America the way than was Mole (5/27). Although we naturally trust our elected leaders, Kelly said on another occasion (5/26), we could be "done in" by them, too. The best way of

dealing with bullies like Mole and Malarkey, Pogo says, is to ignore them (5/30).

Meanwhile, Malarkey, faced with a number of swamp creatures who claim they aren't birds, undertakes corrective action: "We'll jes' get some feathers an' some boilin' tar," says Malarkey, "an' with a little judicious application we can make the creature into any bird we chooses — all nice and neat" (5/16).

At one satiric stroke, Kelly equated McCarthyism with an appropriately belittling analogue, tar-and-feathering — a primitive method of ostracizing that is universally held in low repute. In the delicious finale, Deacon, horrified by what he sees the Bird Watchers Club becoming, shoves Malarkey into the kettle of tar (6/4). Allegorical translation: those who seek to smear others are likely to be tarred with their own brush.

It was as neat a piece of satire as had ever been attempted on the comics pages or anywhere. And the success of it depended upon Kelly's plumbing the potential of his medium to its utmost. Word and picture worked in perfect concert: neither meant much when taken by itself, but when blended, the verbal and the visual achieved allegorical impact and a powerful satiric thrust.

Kelly was to deploy these weapons again and again during the next twenty years. And all of the satiric action took place seemingly without the characters themselves being aware of it: the graphic portrayal of these denizens of the swamp as soft, plastic and harmless joined the vaudevillian strain of the strip to proclaim the essential innocence of the characters, who went about their business, playing at being people, without being conscious of the larger, satiric implications of the acts. The result was a tour de force: humor at each of two levels — one vaudevillian, the other satirical. At times, the stories took on an allegorical cast; at times, the whimsical innocence of the creatures emerged as poignant commentary on the human condition.

Pogo opened, to a greater extent than ever, the possibilities for political and social satire in comic strips. Many strips since *Pogo's* beginnings (*Li'l Abner*, for example) have made their satirical barbs a little sharper. And without *Pogo*, we'd surely have no *Doonesbury*. Garry Trudeau was able to name names in his strip because Kelly had broken the ground, his survival proving that it could be done. And so in the next generation, Trudeau did it in *Doonesbury*. And even Cathy Guisewite did it in *Cathy* (briefly, terribly briefly, before her syndicate commanded her to stick to diet jokes). And although Berke Breathed's satire in *Bloom County* was not as politically pointed as Trudeau's, Breathed was able to dare subjects and attitudes that, before Trudeau (and therefore before Kelly), would have been impossible.

Back in 1953, Kelly wound up his allegory with a stunning shift of mood. Malarkey's menace turns deadly on 6/8, and on the next three installments, Kelly successfully converts his warm and friendly swampland into a dank and sinister place, a genuinely frightening venue — a trick as accomplished as his satire the week before. It was a cartooning *tour de force,* but Kelly was not done yet with McCarthy.

On 6/13, Kelly suggests that witch-hunters eventually destroy themselves, and on 7/20, he confirms that prediction. At the same time, perhaps feeling that the blood-thirstiness of the sequence was decidedly off-key in the strip, he restores the ambiance of the swamp by implying that the villains destroyed themselves. The wonderfully named Sarcophagus MacAbre, a regular in the cast, did not soil his feathers with their blood. Only interlopers committed cannibalism. A year later, however, Kelly removed the onus altogether when Malarkey makes an encore appearance in the strip; but that's another story for another time. (And this time, there was outcry against Kelly's campaign among, not the editors, but the publishers of his client newspapers.)

Malarkey would make yet another appearance in 1954, this time in one of the books of *Pogo* material being published by Simon and Schuster. The books of strip reprints that S&S began producing in 1951 were so popular that the demand quickly exceeded the supply of strips. So in 1953, Kelly generated material expressly for book publication in *Uncle Pogo's So-so Stories.* And the next year, he created similar material for *The Pogo Stepmother Goose.* It was in the latter title that Malarkey appeared again — in another carefully honed satirical allegory.

Kelly had ventured cautiously into satire with *So-so Stories.* One of the stories is about Chicken Little, who, enacting fairly exactly the traditional tale, is a perfect stand-in for the alarmists who see communists under every bed — or, in this case, communist inspired disaster falling from the sky. And a text piece entitled "Dog-gone" seems a parable of how freedom of speech can be lost. But both these efforts were heavily veiled exercises. In *Stepmother Goose*, Kelly tore the veil off.

In "The Town at the Edge of the End," a haunting story without any of the swamp critters, only humans, Kelly portrayed a society that, fear driven, creates its own monsters by oppressing all but socially approved behavior among their fellow citizens. And in some of the poems in the book, he alludes to the worry and fear fostered in the Age of Suspicion. But in the book's last piece, "Who Stole the Tarts?" Kelly recycles the concluding trial sequence from Lewis Carroll's *Alice in Wonderland.* Here, he leaves no doubt as to his motive.

Members of the swampland cast take parts in the production: Pogo is Alice, Albert is the Gryphon, Houn'dog, the Mad Hatter; Deacon Mushrat, the Queen of Hearts. The King, acting as judge in the trial, is played with glowering menace by Malarkey, but here the McCarthy likeness is more pronounced than ever before. And the nonsense routines of the Carroll's courtroom — "Sentence first, verdict later" — give satirical expression to the methods of McCarthyism.

In his "Afterword," Kelly ruminated on the feverish temper of the times:

"Amid the angry demands that our probers behave like 'gentlemen,' let the words of [boxing] Champion James J. Corbett be recalled. Asked why, when abused in a saloon, he acted like a gentleman, he replied: 'Because I can afford to.' There is the answer in a nutshell: Not all of us can afford to. In fact, not all of us can afford to be in saloons in the first place. . . . The moment to call a spade a spade is when we are digging a hole. Such wild life as we encounter in the delving will be ruthlessly identified. If, as we hack through the roots of our trees to find the crawling vermin, we unearth a few trembling, white and guiltless grubs, it cannot be helped. For one cartoonist, the ringing words of the Senatorial Spokesman form a pledge for all seekers of the truth: 'IF ANY STUPID, ARROGANT OR WITLESS MAN APPEARS BEFORE THIS BAR, HE WILL BE EXPOSED.'"

And in *Ten Ever-lovin' Blue-eyed Years with Pogo*, Kelly gave vent again to his disappointment in the more gutless of his fellow citizens: "There was a time in the proud days between 1948 and 1956 when a great many of us in this land of the free and home of the brave were anything but either. . . . Those years were our own fault, not the fault of any one individual or group, and years like them will be our fault again. As I stand here on this platform, I hold between thumb and forefinger a nose that remembers a list of many, many more than 205 belly-whopping heroes who sledded out of sight in the yellow gloom of that gathering wintry dark.

"Properly pressed, we can all remember individual contributors to the shame of the years. We blame several advertisers for withdrawing their support of TV shows that protested against our un-American activities; we blame certain dismal desert stretches of the Press. . . . In these latter more or less golden days of happy preoccupation with other greeds and other envies, we should remember this. We confounded our friends abroad and dumfounded our enemies at home."

We have had ample occasion since to realize that in the conduct of our public and political affairs we have not, apparently, learned much from the lessons of the McCarthy years except the lessons that McCarthy himself embodied. We're still pretty good at throwing political mud, and the news media is still fanatically cooperative.

But in the comic strip *Pogo* during the remainder of the summer of 1953, Kelly refrained from throwing anything more but a party. The allegory finished, he resorted to his usual vaudevillian bag of verbal and visual tricks, returning the strip to the realm of gentle laughter that he had briefly — but oh, so effectively — played hooky from. He indulged his penchant for leap-frogging verbal hijinks (6/29, 7/10), pure nonsense (7/28, 8/6-7) and ingenious sight gags (6/l7, 7/2). And with the "Louisiana perches," Kelly's cast was once again comfortably adrift on a flotilla of puns and double entendres and verbiage taken literally and therefore perversely misunderstood, which only occasionally led to a comment on the passing scene. But that memorable spring of 1953, Kelly had learned how to make his jokes smart, and he would do it again, before McCarthy upstaged himself and unintentionally brought about his own downfall.

From *The Pogo Stepmother Goose*

The Cast

In our continuing effort to learn just how many characters Kelly employed in the swamp, here are listed, in the order of appearance, those who made their first appearance in this volume (bringing the cast total to 133):

Picayune Frog
Halpha Amoeba (Halpha 2 Omeeba)
Roogey Batoon
Flim, Flam and Flo (the Louisiana "perches," who don't actually appear in the strip but are too deliciously named to ignore in any roster such as this one)

MARCH 16, 1953

MARCH 17, 1953

1

MARCH 18, 1953

MARCH 19, 1953

MARCH 20, 1953

MARCH 21, 1953

POGO

by Walt Kelly

MARCH 23, 1953

MARCH 24, 1953

MARCH 25, 1953

MARCH 26, 1953

POGO by Walt Kelly

MARCH 27, 1953

MARCH 28, 1953

POGO by Walt Kelly

MARCH 30, 1953

I WON'T *THREATEN* YOU, MR. OWL. BUT HERE IS A BOOK THAT SAYS: OWLS MIGRATE NORTH ABOUT APRIL FIRST... YOU GOT A DAY TO PACK.

WHY, *YOU* JES' WRIT **THAT** YOU' OWN SELF .... *WHERE'S CAPTAIN WIMBY'S BIRD ATLAS?*

DISCREDITED

IT DIDN'T AGREE WITH OUR OBSERVATIONS... DID IT, MEN?

NO SIR, IT'S OUT OF DATE... *AND* ON FIRE.

THERE'S NOTHING QUITE SO LOVELY AS A BRIGHTLY BURNING BOOK.

MARCH 31, 1953

YOU SEED OL' *MOLE MacCARONY*, THE NATURAL BORN BIRD WATCHER?

YUP..... AN' WORSE LUCK.....

HE SAWN *ME*.

HE IDENTIFIES *ME* AS A BULLFINCH

ALL TWO OR THREE FEET OF ME.

THAT'S A LOT OF BULL-FINCH

CAN'T *YOU* GIT A RECOUNT?

WOOY

LEASTWISE *YOU* **IS** A BIRD~~ HE'S CALLIN'*ME* A **SWALLER** TAILED CUMBERBUND...*ME* AS AIN'T HARDLY A BIRD ATALL

BY JING, IF FROGS HAD **TEETH** HE'D OF BEEN A *GONER!*

AS IT WAS, I GUMMED HIM A *WICKED* ONE ON THE GREAT TOE.

YOU OUGHT TO GO ON HOME AN' WASH OUT YO' MOUTH OUT.

APRIL 1, 1953

APRIL 2, 1953

APRIL 3, 1953

APRIL 4, 1953

POGO by Walt Kelly

APRIL 6, 1953

APRIL 7, 1953

APRIL 8, 1953

I GOT A *MIND* TO **SUE** YOU... PUP DOG LOST HIS VOICE FOR YOUR OL' TEEVY SHOW!

WE COULD **SUE YOU!** WE LISTENED FOR **NOTHIN'**... WE DIN'T TAKE THAT TEEVY JOB. PUP BARKED UP THE WRONG THREE.

SPEAKIN' OF *T.V.*

OLD DAVE TAYLOR

4-8 DIST. BY POST-HALL SYNDICATE

A FRIEND OF MINE MADE A MACHINE THAT SITS AN' WATCHES *T.V.* FOR YOU... **ALL** EVENING... SO'S A BODY CAN GET OUT OF THE HOUSE... *A TEEVY SITTER* HE CALLED IT.... TOOK IT UP TO **N.B.C.**....

FIGGERED IT WOULD EMANCIPATE THE **FAMILY** AND **STILL** NOT WASTE THE SET.... WELL, SIR, THE BOARD OF *DIRECTORS* REFUSED TO LISTEN TO A *MOUSE*... THERE WAS A CRY OF: "*ARE WE MICE OR MEN?!*" IN THE PRO AND CON DISCUSSION WHICH FOLLOWED, AN OLD *EX-DISNEY* MAN TOOK OFFENSE AND TRAMPLED THE **PLANS** INTO PORRIDGE.

COPR. 1953 WALT KELLY

I DON'T KNOW WHY HE WENT TO A **BISCUIT** COMPANY ANYWAY... SWEET TOOTH NO DOUBT. *...WHAT HO!*

CLUNK

OWL'S PRACTICIN' MIGRATIN'...

A OPEN COUNTRY MAN.

OLD DAVE TAYLOR

APRIL 9, 1953

MY FRIEND, OWL, IS *PRACTICIN'* UP ON HIS *MIGRATIN'* AN' SO I COME OVER TO READ A POEM ON TEEVY

VERY GOOD, SIR. WHAT KIND OF AN **OWL** ARE **YOU**?

4-9 DIST. BY POST-HALL SYND.

THE POEM GOES..... UH.. *I* AIN'T NO **OWL**... I AIN'T EVEN A BIRD.....

WERE YOU EVER A BIRD... OR ARE YOU THINKING OF BECOMING ONE?

WULL *SOMEBODY* TOLE ME THAT **REPTILES** ONE TIME CHANGED INTO **BIRDS**, BUT I DON'T THINK I'LL ...

(*PUT HIM DOWN AS A COMMON UPSTART*...... AND HAND ME THAT DISINFECTANT.) **ALL** RIGHT, SIR, LET'S HEAR THE **POEM**.

THE POEM GOES... *ACK! COFF! GUG* KOFF KOFF KAK *UCK·AWF... HARGH! YOWK!*

YOUR POEM IS **VERY** *AMATEURISH!* NO RHYME, SIR. I ADVISE YOU TO **MIGRATE** WITH THE OTHER OWL.

COPR. 1953 WALT KELLY

APRIL 10, 1953

APRIL 11, 1953

APRIL 13, 1953

APRIL 14, 1953

APRIL 15, 1953

APRIL 16, 1953

APRIL 17, 1953

IF, AS IT SEEMS, YOU'RE THINKIN' OF BEIN' A *T.V.* CENSOR AN' A *BORDER GUARD*, BARRIN' BIRDS AN' ALL, I GOT A POEM HERE MIGHT HELP YOU *WEIGH* THE *PROBLEM*.

FINE.

"Give me your tired, your poor, Your huddled masses yearning to breathe free, The wretched refuse of your teeming shore. Send these, the homeless, tempest-tost, to me, I lift my lamp beside the golden door."

WELL... WHAT'S *THAT* ALL ABOUT?

'AT'S BY MIZ LAZARUS, BLESS HER HEART... AN' IT'S ABOUT OUR *SWAMP*...OUR HOME.. WHERE WE DON'T BAR THE DOOR...WHERE WE KEEPS A *EXTRA* FISH IN THE POT FOR STRAY COMP'NY...

A DOOR CLOSES ON *TWO* SIDES.. REMEMBER THAT.

COME! COME! NO NONSENSE VERSE ON OUR *TV* SHOW... CAN YOU DANCE, ACT, SING OR IMITATE A *LOCOMOTIVE* WHISTLE?

IF SO, BLOW.

APRIL 18, 1953

TRY THAT POEM AGAIN. NOT SURE IF I GOT IT ALL.

Give me your tired, your poor, Your huddled masses yearning to breathe free, The wretched refuse of your teeming shore.

Send these, the homeless, tempest-tost, to me, I lift my lamp beside the golden door.

HMM.... WHERE'D YOU SAY YOU GOT THAT?

WELL, A NICE LADY NAME OF EMMA LAZARUS *WRIT* IT-—.BUT I GOT IT OFF'N *ANOTHER* LADY...A *OLD* LADY, STANDIN' OUT IN THE BAY.... *NIGHT* AN' *DAY*---A LADY CARRYIN' A BIG *FLAMIN' TORCH.*

I'M AFRAID YOU *DOVES* ARE RIGHT... HE'S *CRAZY*...OR THE OL' *WOMAN* IS: OUT IN THE WATER IN ALL WEATHER, *ARMED* WITH A *TORCH!* HAH! A PYROMANIAC, NO DOUBT.' A *DANGER* TO ALL.

NO! NOT A OL' MAN WHAT CAN'T SEE..

BUT HE'S TALKIN' 'BOUT THE WOMAN I LOVE.

APRIL 20, 1953

APRIL 21, 1953

APRIL 22, 1953

HOW RIDICKLE·MOUS OF ME TO GIT MAD AT OL' HOUN'DOG 'FORE I EVEN TALKS TO HIM.

THERE'S NO REASON YET TO THINK HE WON'T HELP THROW MOLE OUT.... HE WON'T CLAIM TO BE TOO BUSY... HE WON'T ACT BOSSY... I GOT NO RIGHT TO GIT BURNED OFF....

I'LL WALK UP TO MY OLD PAL KNOWIN' HE'LL HELP....ABLE TO COUNT ON HIM ~ I'LL SHAKE HAN'S AN' EVEN 'FORE I CAN GIT THE WORDS OUTEN MY MOUTH..

LIKE AS NOT THE BANG-BANG CRITTUR WILL REFUSE TO LISTEN!

APRIL 23, 1953

HOUN'DOG ~ YOU IS JES' THE MAN I IS LOOKIN' FOR.

AHA!

YES?

I NEEDS A CANNY·DATE FOR A DANGEROUS MISSION.... CARE TO TOSS YO' HAT IN THE RING?

NO!

BY GEO. Y. WELLS! I KNOWED YOU WOULD BACK OFF, SKEERT!

THAT WASN'T ME! I RENTED THE UPPER STOREY TO LI'L' OL' MOUSE AN' HE'S SENS-ITIVE 'BOUT ME THROWIN' THE HAT ANYWHERE.

APRIL 24, 1953

APRIL 25, 1953

18

POGO
by Walt Kelly

APRIL 27, 1953

THE REASON I RENTED THE HAT WAS 'CAUSE THE *MOLE* TOLD ME TO MIGRATE.

CLAIMED YOU WAS A *FLAM*INGO, HUH?

YEP.... HE SAID ALL THE FLAMINGOS WERE HEADIN' FOR THE *DERBY*.... TOLD ME I HAD TO WORK AT CHURCHILL DOWNS... *ME*, AS CAN'T OUT-RUN A *POTATO* BUG .....*HA!* I'M A FULL BLOODIED AMERICAN RODENT BY TRADE AN' *PROUD* OF IT.

NO DAG BLAGGIN' SELF-APPOINTED COP KIN PUSH *ME* AROUND.....I SWORE I, FOR *ONE*, WAS GONNA STAND *FIRM!* UNFEARED! CONFIDENT OF MY *RIGHTS!* SO I TOOK A ASSUMED NAME AN' HID IN THE HAT.

HE'S *RIGHT!* ARE WE *MICE* OR ARE WE *MEN?*

COPR. 1953 WALT KELLY

APRIL 28, 1953

THE *NOBLE DOG* DON'T THINK *HIDIN'* IS THE WAY TO HANDLE THE PROBLEM OF THE MOLE.

RIGHT.

BUT...

THE THING TO DO IS STAY OUT IN THE *OPEN* LIKE A *HONEST MAN!* YOU GOT A RIGHT TO ENJOY *FREEDOM.* THE MOLE, YOU GOTTA ADMIT, IS *ANYWAY* NEARSIGHTED..

AN' IF YOU RUNS ACROSS HIM IN THE 'COURSE OF THE DAY ... A LITTLE PRUDENT *TIPPY-TOEIN'* WILL, IN ALL PROLLIBILITY, GIT YOU BY *UN*-NOTICED.....

COPR. 1953 WALT KELLY

APRIL 29, 1953

WHAT'S THE DIFFERMINTS 'TWEEN HIDIN' AN' SNEAKIN' TO AVOID THE MOLE?

VERY WELL, I WILL FACE HIM... BEGUILE HIM... SPEAK TO HIM WITH CHARM. TROUBLE IS: YOU CRITTURS CAN'T HANDLE CULTURE.

SOME OF YOU BIRDS DESERVE TO BE UNDENTIFIED... IF YOU GOT NOTHIN' TO HIDE. STEP UP, SPEAK AS ONE GENTLEMAN TO ANOTHER... HEH-LO THERE, SIR!

YOU LOOKS JUST FINE TODAY... I'M...

...A UNEMPLOYED BIRD DOG... A BASSET HOUN' PERCHANCE OR MIXED AFGHAN... MAYBE A MONGRELOID IDIOT OR A GRIFFONISH POODLE... YOU'LL NEVER DO TO WATCH BIRDS... TOO RISKY..

MIGHT WATCH ONLY YOUR FAVORITE BIRD... QUAIL OR PTMARMIMMLEGAN OR PHILADELPHILIA VIREO... YOUR BACKGROUND IS QUESTIONABLE SIR... GOOD DAY.

APRIL 30, 1953

WELL, DID THE MOLE UNDENTIFY YOU POLITE LIKE?

HE DIN'T UNDENITTIFY ME AT ALL... A CRUEL BLOW TO ONE OF HIGH PEDIGREE... AN' A INSULT TO MAN'S BEST FRIENDS EVERYWHERE.

MY FAMILY TREE IS ONE OF THIS COUNTRY'S VERY CHARTER OAKS... EVEN IN A SPOTTY YEAR I ONCE WON A SET OF WHITE WALL TIRES FROM THE DALMATIAN CLUB OF AMERICA. AYE... RIBBONS GALORE.

MY GYPSY FOREBEARS RAN WITH THE ROMANIES... THRU THE AGES... KNOWED AS THE PLUM PUDDIN' DOG... THE FIRE HOUSE DOG... WITHOUT US THE CHICAGO FIRE WOULD BE UNSUNG!

THEM'S ALL SPOT DOGS. WHERE'S YOUR SPOTS?

THE VOLSTEAD ACT... PATER WAS REDUCED TO A DIET OF SPOT REMOVER... AN' BECOME KNOWED AS "OLD PAINT" OR "RING TING TING", A NOISE IN TH' HEAD WHO WAS A FAMOUS HORSEPLAYER (OR COWBOY) IN THE EARLY FILM INDUSTRY.

UM.

POGO

by Walt Kelly

MAY 1, 1953

MAY 2, 1953

MAY 4, 1953

PHOO! A NAPOLEONIC RETREAT BEFORE WE EVEN SEED A FLAKE OF MUSCOVY SNOW.

PRUDENCE! PRUDENCE! DISCREDENCE IS A BETTER PART THAN VALOR.

YOU BIG TANKERS IS TAKIN' A **DIVE** WITHOUT CLIMBIN' INTO THE RING... JES' CAUSE THAT **SIMPLE J. MALARKEY** GOT A SHOT GUN.... **I'M GOIN' BACK..** I'M TOO SMALL A TARGET TO BOTHER WITH...

'COURSE THIS MALARKEY FELLA IS A BACKWOODS **FELINE**... FIGHTS WITH THE FINESSE AN' FAIR PLAY OF A FEMALE **FOSSA**---- **AND** HAS A SWEET TOOTH FOR **MICE!**

WELL, I ADMIRE HIS **TASTE**, BUT I THINK IT'S ILLEGAL....SO I WON'T COUNTERBUTE TO THE DELINQUENCY OF A MINOR (IN CASE **HE'S UNDER AGE**).. I'LL STEP OFF A WAYS AN' LOOK UP THE STATUTES AN'...

MAY 5, 1953

Fellow Bird Watchers, we are met today to welcome a new member, Simple J. Malarkey

Anyone with as much Birding experience as Mr. Malarkey should have an interesting record ---- So, unless there is an objection.. I will read an account of his past ~~

-- activities

BAM

objection sustained, Mr. Malarkey.

WELCOME TO THE CLUB, SIMPLE J.

22

POGO
by Walt Kelly

MAY 6, 1953

Panel 1: FRIENDS, I IS MOUGHTY PROUD YOU IS VOTED ME INTO THE CLUB AN' NOW THAT I IS IN CHARGE I'M GONNA CHANGE THE NAME AN'.....

Panel 2: In all due respect, Mr. Simple J. Malarkey, nobody voted you to the leadership -- and the name we have is quite satisfactory.....

Panel 3: BETSEY, HERE, GOT SIX OR SEVEN VOTES IN HER ALONE. BUT STOP THE WAYWARD BICKERING... *STICK TO FACTS!* I'M PRESIDENT... THAT MUCH IS CLEAR... WE CAN COUNT VOTES LATER.

Panel 4: WE'LL **TABLE** YOUR QUIBBLING AN' *PROCEED*... THE NAME OF THE UNIT IS CHANGED TO THE "*BONFIRE BOYS*"... RIGHT?

NO NO NO **NO**

FINE..."BONFIRE BOYS" IT IS!

HOW YOU STARTS A BONFIRE?

BY RUBBIN' OL' MEMBERS THE WRONG WAY.

MAY 7, 1953

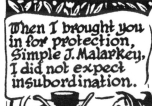

Panel 1: When I brought you in for protection, Simple J. Malarkey, I did not expect insubordination.

AW, DEACON, PAL... LOOK AT IT THE *HONEST* WAY.... I'M IN CHARGE, DEAC', *HOW* CAN I BE INSUBORDINATE?

Panel 2: The Constitution of the Bird Watchers Club guarantees Free Elections --- *you can't just bull your way into the Presidency!*

AW, PLEASE BE QUIET, DEAC'!

Panel 3: Me keep quiet?! This constitution also guarantees my right to speak up...Right there, you Usurper!

SURE, PAL, SURE ---- BUT, GOSH DEAC' BOY, NO SET OF RULES CAN DO ONE THING, PAL.

Panel 4: IT CAN'T GUARANTEE WHAT WILL HAPPEN *AFTER* A GUY SPEAKS UP......*YOU* BEEN SPEAKIN' UP GOOD, DEAC', BUT GOSH, FELLA, IT DON'T PAY TO TINKER FOREVER WITH CHANCE HA HA LIKE THE FELLA SAYS.

23

MAY 8, 1953

MAY 9, 1953

POGO

by Walt Kelly

MAY 11, 1953

MAY 12, 1953

MAY 13, 1953

MAY 14, 1953

POGO by Walt Kelly

MAY 15, 1953

THAT **CLEOPATRA LURE** WAS TOO RISKY... I BETTER STICK TO BEIN' A **OUT-OF-WORK WAIF** AN' GO ASK 'EM FOR A **JOB.**

AYE ~. THE FUNNY [SIC] PAPER ALLUS HANDLES IT THAT WAY.

THIS DOG BONE THING CALLED "**POGGO**" IS JES' ABOUT INCOMPREE-HENSIBULE.

GOOD LUCK! US'LL COME A-RUNNIN' WHEN YOU IS NEEDY.

SIMPLE J., YOUR METHODS ARE TOO CRUDE ... YOU SHOULD HAVE **DIGNITY** AND **LAW** ON YOUR SIDE. YOU CAN'T JUST **SAY** YOU'RE BOSS.

YES, I CAN, PAL...I GOT A **LOT** OF **VOTES** IN OL' BETSEY HERE. **THAT'S** LAW.

BASIC LAW SAYS "**NO!**", FRIEND. YOU **HAVE NO** CONSTITUENCY... I REMOVED THE VOTES WHILE YOU WERE NAPPING....LUCKILY, THEY FIT MY **SAWED OFF MODEL** A PARLIAMENTARY POINT THAT CAN NOT BE OVERLOOKED.

UM.

MAY 16, 1953

HMMPH!

HAIL, FRIENDS! I AM A LORN ORPHAN IN NEED OF SCULLERY WORK, HARDSHIP AND OTHER DRUDGERY AN'..

WHAT KIND OF A **BIRD** IS **YOU?**

BUT... I'M NOT A **BIRD**, SIRS... NOT **REALLY**.... I'M A POOR LOST ORPHAN LIKE I SAID...

NOT A **BIRD** AT ALL? **IMPOSSIBLE** ...

OH, WE CAN FIX THAT, HON. MOLE .....WE'LL JES' GIT SOME **FEATHERS** AN' SOME ...

BOILIN' TAR, AN' WITH A LITTLE JUDICIOUS APPLICATION WE CAN MAKE THE CHILD INTO **ANY BIRD** WE CHOOSES .....**ALL NICE AND NEAT**....

ALL VERY NICE AND NEAT

POGO

Walt Kelly

MAY 18, 1953

MAY 19, 1953

28

POGO
by Walt Kelly

MAY 20, 1953

MAY 21, 1953

POGO

by Walt Kelly

MAY 22, 1953

MAY 23, 1953

oop! this-un's 3-26 again!

31

POGO

by Walt Kelly

MAY 29, 1953

MAY 30, 1953

33

JUNE 1, 1953

JUNE 2, 1953

by Walt Kelly

JUNE 3, 1953

JUNE 4, 1953

JUNE 5, 1953

JUNE 6, 1953

POGO

by Walt Kelly

JUNE 8, 1953

JUNE 9, 1953

JUNE 10, 1953

JUNE 11, 1953

JUNE 12, 1953

JUNE 13, 1953

POGO

by Walt Kelly

JUNE 15, 1953

JUNE 16, 1953

POGO *by* Walt Kelly

JUNE 17, 1953

I THINK I GOT THE **NEW CALENDAR** *ALL* SET.

NEW CALENDAR?

YEP... THE **OCTOBER CALENDAR**... CHRISTMAS COMES ON THE **86**TH OF OCTOBER.

ONE GOOD MONTH ALL YEAR LONG. THE **FIRST** OF THE YEAR FALLS ON OCTOBER NINETY-THIRD... WODDY YOU THINK OF THAT!

OH, I DUNNO.....IT'S ONE OF THEM THINGS I DON'T THINK ABOUT VERY MUCH.

JUNE 18, 1953

YOU SUGGESTED THAT THE WHOLE YEAR BE **OCTOBER**, MAKIN' **NEW YEAR'S DAY** COME **WHEN?**

THE HON. GEO. WARD

ON THE NINETY-THIRD OF OCTOBER.

THAT'S RIDICULOUS! **HOW** CAN THE **FIRST** DAY OF THE YEAR COME ON THE **NINETY-THIRD?**

GEO. WARD

SHEER COINCIDENCE.

SOMETIMES I DON'T FOLLOW YOU AN' SO FAR IT **ALLUS** HAS PAID OFF.

THE HON.

POGO

by Walt Kelly

JUNE 19, 1953

JUNE 20, 1953

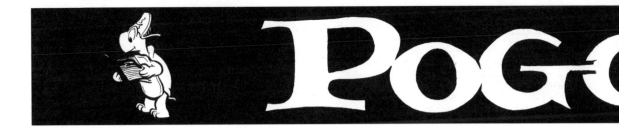

POGO

by Walt Kelly

JUNE 22, 1953

SO YOU IS THE PICAYUNE FROG?

YEP... A FREE LANCE FORE-CASTER.

HEY, PORKY, I IS CHANGIN' THE WHOLE YEAR INTO OCTOBER! REE-VOLUTIONIZIN' THE CALENDAR.

IT REMIND ME OF A ELDERLY JEST: A OCTOBER CALENDAR IS EASY TO USE COZ IN OCTOBER THE LEAVES TURN THEMSELVES... HA-HA?

OH, YES YES, YES INDEED.

I HEARD A JOKE, OWL. AN' I IS WILLIN' TO REGALE YOU. A OCTOBER CALENDAR IS EASY TO USE BECAUSE THE TREES CHANGE COLORS AT THAT TIME OF YEAR.

AND—?

AND A MOST BEAUTIFUL SIGHT IT IS INDEED!

JUNE 23, 1953

THIS NEW ORLEANS PAPER HELD A CONTEST TO SEE WHO'D BE THE WEATHER MAN... ME OR A OUTLANDER NAMED "POGO" (SAID TO HAVE SHARP WEATHER EARS.)

HA! ME AN' OL' GEORGE, THE HEAD MAN, FIXED THAT! WE BOLSTERED THE BALLOT BOX AN' I WAS A SHOO IN!.....ONLY LATER DID I LEARN THAT THE JOB CARRIED NO SALARY.

I DENOUNCED THIS PENURIOUS ATTITUDE AND FOUND MYSELF AT LIBERTY... SO I PICKETED THE MARDI GRAS SINGLEHANDED... GEORGE CHARGED THAT I WAS NOT A FROG BUT A MIDGET ALLIGATOR! A VILE SLANDER!

ON WHO, HOPPY TOES?

43

JUNE 24, 1953

JUNE 25, 1953

JUNE 26, 1953

JUNE 27, 1953

45

POGO
by Walt Kelly

JUNE 29, 1953

JUNE 30, 1953

POGO
by Walt Kelly

JULY 1, 1953

A REAL EMERGENCY... A JOB FOR THE *GLEE, PERLOO AN' FIRE SOCIETY*--- HEY! HEY!

ONE AT A TIME, SIR... WE'RE UP AGAINST ONE PROBLEM, NOW.

AH...

JUMP JUMP JUMP JUMP JUMP JUMP JUMP JUMP JUMP JUMP

WELL, WE GOT NO MORE TIME FOR CHILDREN'S GAMES. *NOW THEN, POGO, WHAT'S ON YOUR MIND?*

FIRE!

DING DANG BLING BLANG !?!

JULY 2, 1953

Poisoning is too good for those two usurpers--- eh-- What's that?

URF URF URF

IT'S ME *LAUGHIN'...* I'M BEGINNIN' TO UNDERSTAND THE JOKE YESTERDAY. WISH'T *I* HAD A SENSE OF HUMOR....

How can you simpletons laugh when authority is taken from the hands of the Rightful.?

YOU BRUNG IN THEM TWO EXPERT BIRDWATCHERS.... SAYIN' IT WAS TO KEEP US FROM MAKIN' *DERN FOOLS* OF OURSELFS... WHERE AS IT'S THE *IN*HERENT RIGHT OF *ALL* TO MAKE DERN FOOLS OF THEIR-SELFS...

IT AIN'T A RIGHT HELD BY YOU *OFFICIAL* TYPES ALONE..... THE REST OF US MIGHT NOT HAVE THE SHEER ABILITY AT IT BUT US *DO* GOT THE RIGHT..... SO DON'T MESS WITH IT......

oop again! where 7-2?

47

POGO

by Walt Kelly

JULY 3, 1953

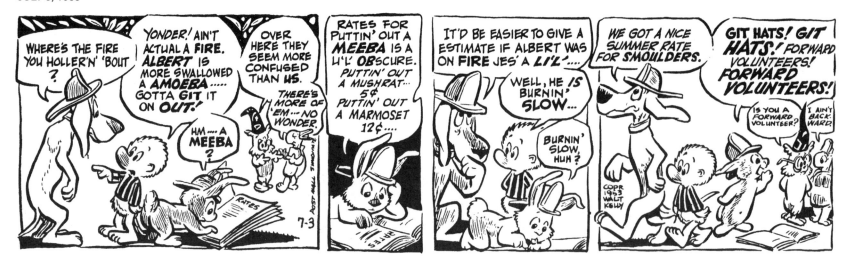

JULY 4, 1953

POGO

by Walt Kelly

JULY 6, 1953

JULY 7, 1953

POGO

by Walt Kelly

JULY 8, 1953

JULY 9, 1953

JULY 10, 1953

JULY 11, 1953

JULY 13, 1953

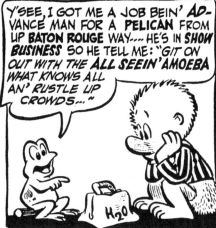
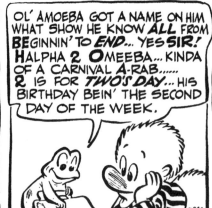

JULY 14, 1953

JULY 15, 1953

JULY 16, 1953

JULY 20, 1953

JULY 21, 1953

JULY 22, 1953

JULY 23, 1953

POGO

by Walt Kelly

JULY 24, 1953

SLUM THAT SAM'WICH DOWN IN BACK OF OWL 'CAUSE HIS FRONT IS TICKLISH..... HOPE YOU PUT PLENTY ...UH-UH.....

YEH..... I PUT PLENTY.....

UH-UH

--- PEPPER ON IT

JULY 25, 1953

BEE-HOLE, THERE, CAP'N, SIR! ---A BIG UGLY OL' PROJECTILE IS PROJECKIN' OFF'N OF OUR STARBOARN BROW!

HOWDY! US IS FROM SOUTH MARS, FRIEND, MEBBE KIN YOU KINDLY TELL WHUT KIND OF POWER YOU USES?

SHO NUFF.

ALBERT IS SNEEZED ME OUT--- SO I FIGGER I IS USIN' SNEEZE POWER!

US WILL BE DOG BONED!

YOU IS RIGHT, LIEUTENEMENT... THESE HUMANS IS MOUGHTY UGLY AN' RUE-DI-MENTERRY.

MAN! WHUT A STRONG OL' FOREIGN ACCENT THEM MARS CRITTURS GOT.

JULY 27, 1953

HERE I IS **STILL** FLYIN' THRU THE AIR AFTER **ALBERT** SNUZ ME OUTEN HIS CRAW.

7-27

STAN' BACK, PORKY... I GOTTA PRACTICE UP ON MY AND OWL'S DUEL IN **ALBERT'S** HONOR.

SNEAK UP ON THE TARGET AN' **DAG** IT BY SURPRISE.

POST HALL SYNDICATE

I WAS FIGGERIN' ON **INTRODUCIN'** GERM WARFARE... IT WOULD BE VERY **WHIMSICAL**... .....KNOW ANY **GERMS?** ----OUCH!

I WINS! I **PEARLED** YO' HARBOR, SON.

I WIN! HE WHO SNEAKS TH' FIRST BLOW IS **LOST** THE ARGUMINTS.

GOTTA DO A- NOTHER WAR TO SEE WHO WON THE LAST 'UN?

COPR. 1953 WALT KELLY

JULY 28, 1953

WHAT?

YEAH...WHAT?

BACK TO THE FIRE! BACK TO THE FIRE!

I CARRY THE **HOSE!**

7-28 POST HALL SYNDICATE

WHAT·D·YA MEAN? *BACK TO THE FIRE?*

WE TOOK THE WEEK-END OFF. *UNION HOURS* Y'KNOW.

I CARRY THE HOSE.

NOW IT'S BACK TO THE FIRE... *WHICH WAY,* HORRENDO?

DON'T ASK *ME*... I CARRY THE HOSE.

COPR. 1953 WALT KELLY

58

JULY 29, 1953

JULY 30, 1953

JULY 31, 1953

I IS A-LOOKIN' AT YOU AN' I IS A-FIGGER'N'.

LOOK AWAY, DIXIE LAMB. I CARRY THE HOSE.

THAT'S IT! YOU AN' HOUN'DOG IS RUNNIN' A *FIRE DEEPARTMINT,* BUT YOU **NEITHER** KNOWS WHERE YOU IS *GOIN'* --- WHAT'S YOU GOT TO SAY TO *THAT?*

WELL, I CARRY A HOSE.

WHAT FOR DOES YOU CARRY IT FOR? WHA' FOR?! WHAFFOR?

THAT'S WHAFFER.

AUGUST 1, 1953

HERE'S THE *LAST* OF THE *FISH* YOU FLUNG.

WAIT 'TIL I *TALLY* 'EM UP.

WHAT'S YOU GOTTA *TALLY* UP? THEY WAS ONLY *THREE.*

NOW! NOW! YOU IS GIVE ME **TWO** ... **THIS** ONE MAKES *THREE.*

HOLD HIM A MINUTE .... WHERE'S THE OTHER TWO --- AH, HERE --- WELL, *THAT ONE IS THREE* .. SO THIS ONE IS *FOUR* --- THIS ONE IS *FIVE* ...

SIX.

SEE! *SIX!* IT PAYS TO TALLY UP, HOUN'DOG... DON'T IT NOW?

60

POGO

by Walt Kelly

AUGUST 5, 1953

AUGUST 6, 1953

AUGUST 7, 1953

HEY! ALBERT!

SOMETHIN' IS STRUCK ME, POGO..... LET'S BEAT IT!

LET'S.

8-7

GOOD! WE IS EXCAPIN' SO FAST I IS ALMOST LOSIN' MY HAT!

HOT DOG!

POST HALL SYNDICATE.

HAT? I AIN'T GOT NO HAT.

HEY!

COPR. 1953 WALT KELLY

THEY IS COME FOR US, POGO.

AUGUST 8, 1953

POGO, TELL ALBERT WE AIN'T SUPER. NATURAL

LOOKIN' AT YO' FRIEND I B'LEEVE THAT IS HARD TO B'LEEVE.

DIN'T YOU IS EVER SEE A PELICAN AFORE?

8-8

POST HALL SYNDICATE

SURE, FOLKS, THIS HERE IS GOOD OL' ROOGEY BATOON, THE LOU'SIANA TYPE PELICAN.

HE'S THE BOY WHAT MADE THE LOU'SIANA PURCHASE.

MY! IS YOU REALLY?

YUP.

YUP.... I MADE ALL THREE OF 'EM.

HUH?

HUH?

HUH?

COPR 1953 WALT KELLY

AUGUST 10, 1953

AUGUST 11, 1953

POGO

by Walt Kelly

AUGUST 12, 1953

AUGUST 13, 1953

65

AUGUST 17, 1953

AUGUST 18, 1953

AUGUST 19, 1953

AUGUST 20, 1953

AUGUST 21, 1953

AUGUST 22, 1953

AUGUST 24, 1953

AUGUST 25, 1953

POGO

by Walt Kelly

AUGUST 26, 1953

AUGUST 27, 1953

POGO

by Walt Kelly